Jesus in Beijing

A Missionary Memoir of Christ's Victory in China

Matt Click

ISBN 979-8-89309-818-1 (Paperback)
ISBN 979-8-89485-397-0 (Hardcover)
ISBN 979-8-89309-819-8 (Digital)

Copyright © 2024 Matt Click
All rights reserved
First Edition

All rights reserved. No part of this publication may be reproduced, distributed, or transmitted in any form or by any means, including photocopying, recording, or other electronic or mechanical methods without the prior written permission of the publisher. For permission requests, solicit the publisher via the address below.

Covenant Books
11661 Hwy 707
Murrells Inlet, SC 29576
www.covenantbooks.com

Dedicated to my missionary friends and colleagues,
whose relentless zeal for Christ inspires me still.

Contents

Foreword vii
Introduction ix

Chapter 1: Happy Life Warning 1
Chapter 2: Knock, Knock 3
Chapter 3: Broken Chains 5
Chapter 4: Doubting Her Doubts 8
Chapter 5: Lunch in the Canteen 10
Chapter 6: Study Break Tears 13
Chapter 7: Lord of the Locusts 16
Chapter 8: The Problem Solver's Wide Web 19
Chapter 9: The Lecture Hall 21
Chapter 10: A Widow's Awful Food and Awesome Prayers 24
Chapter 11: Life-Changing Pepsi 26
Chapter 12: The Gospel in Leviticus 29
Chapter 13: A Taoist Finds Truth 32
Chapter 14: Uncle W and the Dogs 35
Chapter 15: The Summit 38
Chapter 16: Flashback: Blindsided by God's Grace ... 40

Foreword

King Jesus, not Xi Jinping, rules over China.

In 1949, Chairman Mao Zedong began to expel all the Christian missionaries from the newly founded People's Republic of China. Over the next twenty-five years, Mao imposed his tyrannical reign over the Middle Kingdom via the so-called Cultural Revolution and Great Leap Forward. At the time, social scientists and historians outside China supposed Christianity had been completely wiped off the Chinese map.

At Mao's death in 1976, however, as the late Deng Xiaoping reopened China to the outside world, foreign analysts were surprised, even shocked, to discover that during Mao's quarter century of dictatorial rule, somehow, inexplicably, Christianity not only survived but thrived. But it wasn't just the foreign analysts who discovered this surprising truth and trend.

In the early 2000s, the Chinese government, concerned that Christianity in China was on the rise, conducted its own internal audit and discovered, much to its great consternation, that professing Chinese Christians on the mainland outnumbered registered members of the Communist Party. What is more, some reports say the number of Chinese Christians keeps rising. By the year 2050, it is estimated that there will be well over one hundred million Chinese Christians in the Middle Kingdom.

Clearly, Xi Jinping, despite all his draconian crackdowns on Christianity, does not have the upper hand. On the contrary, the Lord Jesus reigns in China.

I experienced something of Christ's victorious reign during my decade-long tenure in China. In the following chapters, I share just a small sampling of these victories. To be clear, these are not all the victories I witnessed. Also, I have intentionally changed the names of everyone whose story I have told in order to protect their identities from a still-hostile government. As a further safety precaution, I have left out location names and time markers. As such, I trust the reader will forgive my deliberate geographical and chronological ambiguity.

Ultimately, I have written this memoir because I believe these stories need to be told. We live in a dark day. It seems at times like Christians are losing the war—as though Christ's kingdom is being repelled by evil. But this simply is not true. Two thousand years ago, King Jesus assured us that the gates of hell would not prevail against his church (Matt. 16:18). This same Jesus, after he rose from the dead and just prior to his ascension, gave marching orders to make disciples of all nations (Matt. 28:19). Jesus mandated the mission, and Christ's mission, under his divine authority, will not fail.

Introduction

The pulled pork sandwich proved less memorable than the life-altering conversation it produced.

No one at the Lone Star State restaurant's long light-beige table likely noticed, or even cared, that at least two in the group were talking about something entirely different from the subject matter that had brought them all together in the first place.

The majority of the group, made up mostly of prospective seminary students, chatted about such topics as tuition, campus life, local ministry opportunities, and so on. After all, this was supposed to be a seminary campus tour—not exactly a world tour.

But I must have missed the memo.

"So what do you do at the school?" I asked the man seated directly across from me. I assumed he was on staff at the seminary.

"I'm the director of the seminary missions center," he replied, taking a quick bite of his sandwich.

"That's cool," I said. "I guess you see a lot of neat stuff going on all around the world, huh?"

I casually began to sink my teeth into the mouth-watering Texas meat.

"Actually," he said, "God is doing some pretty amazing things all around the world."

"Really? Like what kind of things?" I asked, half-forgetting about my pulled pork.

For the next several minutes, the mission director—to this day, I honestly don't remember his first or last name—told me stories of how God was at work all across the globe, from one continent to the next. He testified of peoples and various ethnicities converting to Christ. My heart burned ablaze as he shared.

"Can we talk some more later this afternoon?" I asked.

We agreed that after my campus tour ended, I would go track him down in his office and chat further about these things. When we met up later that afternoon, the man briefly expounded on his previous points, answered my questions, prayed with me, and then handed me a rather tall stack of mission-related materials, which included, of all things, a few VHS tapes.

I went back home to Oklahoma that evening. The next day, I popped in the first VHS tape on top. It was a video all about China, and it described the Middle Kingdom's deep spiritual needs. I was immediately hooked. I knew I wanted to go to China. I knew I *needed* to go to China. Less than twelve months later, I boarded a plane to China.

Chapter 1

Happy Life Warning

> Preach the word; be ready in season and out of season.
> —2 Tim. 4:2 (ESV)

"If you want to live a happy life in this city, you will stop telling others about Jesus."

I sat there dumbfounded. I had visited the local Public Security Bureau (PSB) on this particular day because it was on this day that Officer Han had arranged for me to come by his office to pick up my travel documents, which were in need of renewal.

I had known Officer Han for some time now, approximately one year. He knew I was a Christian. And he also knew I was actively sharing my faith with those around me.

And now, in this moment, I sat in the hot seat across from him and his fellow comrade. A lone desk left little distance between me, the Christian, and this pair of unbelieving Communists.

What would I say? How could I respond? I was there that day, I thought, for my visa, not a grilling. But God had other plans.

The words, *if you want to live a happy life,* hung in the air for several seconds before I finally broke the silence.

"Who, then, can I tell about Jesus?" I asked nervously.

"Well," said Officer Han matter-of-factly, "you can tell your very close friends."

Suddenly, I realized this was my golden opportunity. In China, life is all about *guanxi*, that is, connections or relationships. To have *guanxi* in China matters because to the Chinese, relationships matter. It's not *what* you know; it's *who* you know. You can get anything done at any time, anywhere, no matter the cost, if you have the right relationships.

"Officer Han," I said, in a direct but respectful tone, "we've known each other for close to a year now. Would you say we are close friends?"

"Oh yes, yes, of course," he said, nodding in approval. "We are good friends."

Not missing my chance, I popped the question.

"Since we are such good friends, can I tell *you* about Jesus while I'm here today?"

"Sure, that's fine. Go right ahead," he said.

So right then and there, in the confines of the local police headquarters in Communist China, I proceeded to share the gospel with Officer Han and his colleague.

Neither one of them became a Christian that day. In fact, both men flatly rejected my message. But somehow—despite their warning and subsequent rejection—I felt that day a rising courage deep in my soul to want to speak all the more boldly for the name of Christ. And yet somehow, I knew I wasn't the only one.

Chapter 2

Knock, Knock

Count it all joy, my brothers, when you meet trials of various kinds.
—Jas. 1:2

The knock on my apartment door was unexpected.

It was the middle of the afternoon. My roommate and I were home at the time, resting a bit after a long morning of Mandarin language studies.

Who was it at the door this time? Probably just the neighborhood kids wanting to play soccer with the white-faced foreigners. *Come on, kiddos,* I thought. *I'm no star athlete. Just let me rest.*

Hence, I was not prepared for who stood on the other side of the door—or, worse yet, who *wasn't* standing on the other side of the door.

I opened the door. It was Mrs. Wang, a dear Chinese-Korean Christian lady, the wife of a missionary evangelist and personal friend of mine. And she was crying profusely.

"My husband is gone," she said through tearful sobs. "The police have taken him away. And I don't know where he is."

Still standing in the doorway, stunned yet not quite sure what to do, my roommate and I motioned Mrs. Wang to come inside.

O Lord, help us, I prayed inwardly as we ushered Mrs. Wang to our living room seating area.

"I'm so, so sorry," I said. "Tell us what happened."

Mrs. Wang explained that her husband had recently been doing quite a bit of traveling in and out of the surrounding villages, sharing the gospel everywhere he went. He had just returned home yesterday from his latest trip. Earlier today, however, the police showed up at their home, arrested him, and confiscated his many Bibles.

Meanwhile, Mrs. Wang, who witnessed her husband's arrest, knew nothing of his current whereabouts. So she came to our apartment, in need of comfort and prayer.

I quickly grabbed my Bible and pointed us to James 1:2–4:

Count it all joy, my brothers, when you meet trials of various kinds, for you know that the testing of your faith produces steadfastness. And let steadfastness have its full effect, that you may be perfect and complete, lacking in nothing.

Easier said than done, I thought. *O Lord, be merciful! Let our brother be released—and quickly.*

After praying with Mrs. Wang, we sent her on her way and assured her that we would keep praying. A few days later, we received yet another knock on our door.

Again, it wasn't the neighborhood kids wanting to play ball. And this time it wasn't even Mrs. Wang.

Instead, it was Mrs. Wang's husband—he had been released from jail.

And now, standing at my door and then seated in my living room, this beloved brother in Christ recounted a most unusual story of God's mercy.

Mrs. Wang's husband shared how shortly after his arrest, the police interrogated him at great length with many questions and threats. But finally, in the end, after our brother courageously and openly admitted to the police that he was an evangelist simply doing God's work and preaching the gospel, the local police bureau issued him an approval letter and instructed him to present that document to the local authorities anytime he traveled in and out of towns to share the gospel.

Truly, I had never seen or heard of anything like this before—and haven't seen anything like this since.

Yet this wouldn't be the only time the Lord blew my mind with his grace, as more grace was on the way.

Chapter 3

Broken Chains

So if the Son sets you free, you will be free indeed.
—John 8:36

It all began with a handwritten note.

One summer, a short-term volunteer team from the American South showed up in my city to work with college students. For the better part of June and July, these USA natives had the opportunity to interact with future teachers in China. The summer made for an interesting cultural exchange of sorts. Both the Americans and the Chinese got to learn about the other's history, religion, customs, heritage, and the like. Naturally, these Americans made it their ambition to share whatever they could, however they could, about their faith in Christ with their new Chinese friends.

At the end of the two-month endeavor, I asked the team to make me a list of names and phone numbers of any of their new Chinese friends they wanted me to follow up with. Maybe it was someone who seemed hungry for spiritual truth. Maybe it was someone who asked good questions.

"Just jot down whoever comes to your mind," I told them. "And I'll follow up as best as I can."

One member of the volunteer team, Luke, gave me a handwritten note which simply read "Yang Yi needs follow-up" and included a local mobile number. After the volunteer team returned to the

United States, I picked up my cell phone and dialed the number next to Yang Yi's name, not sure what to expect. Yang Yi answered the phone, I introduced myself as Luke's friend, and he agreed to meet me later that week for lunch.

When I met him for lunch a few days later, Yang Yi was accompanied by two of his classmates—Lee and Pan.

We talked about all sorts of things. But as was my custom, I wasted little time getting to spiritual matters. I mentioned that my favorite book was the Bible and gave a quick synopsis of the Bible's storyline.

Neither Lee nor Pan appeared overly interested. Yang Yi, however, paid close attention to my words.

Over the next few weeks and months, I continued to meet with Yang Yi. We ate meals together and played basketball. And I kept telling him about the Lord Jesus. Finally, at Christmastime, I invited Yang Yi and his thirty classmates over to my apartment for a party to celebrate the holiday. We fried dumplings, played various icebreaker games, and then I showed his entire class a one-hour film all about Jesus and the gospel. Amazingly, the whole group watched intently—no one messed with his or her cell phone, as all their friends were there together in one room.

A few weeks later, in January, Yang Yi invited me to his hometown village for the Chinese New Year holiday. As we sat around the fire one evening, trying to keep warm in the frigid cold air while his mom cooked dinner, I asked Yang Yi a question.

"Yang Yi, I've been telling you about Jesus for some months now. What do you think about Jesus?"

Yang Yi leaned in with a serious expression and replied, "I believe in Jesus."

Not convinced that we were saying the same thing, I protested. "No, Yang Yi, I don't mean believe, like, know something with one's mind. I'm not talking about simply believing a set of facts. I'm talking about believing in Jesus with all of one's heart and soul."

"I know," Yang Yi said.

And then Yang Yi said something I'll never forget as long as I live.

Crossing his two fists, his left wrist over his right like an X, he said, "Before I believed in Jesus, I was bound to my sin. But now I have believed in Jesus, and he has set me free."

Excited, yet confused, I literally scratched my head.

"I don't get it," I said. "When? Where? How?"

"At your Christmas party," he explained. "You showed us a movie about Jesus. It talked about how Jesus died on the cross and rose again for our sins. At the end of the movie, it said we could pray and ask God to forgive us of our sins if we trusted in Jesus. And I did—that night."

Sure enough, he was serious. Yang Yi did believe in Jesus. A short time later, I baptized him. He was the first in his village to believe in the Lord Jesus. But of course, Yang Yi couldn't keep the gospel to himself. He would go on to share the gospel with his family. Both his parents, his little brother, one of his sisters, and an aunt all turned to the Lord almost immediately following Yang Yi's conversion. Yet not everyone in the family was so easily converted.

Chapter 4

Doubting Her Doubts

> Then he said to Thomas, "Put your finger here, and see my hands; and put out your hand, and place it in my side. Do not disbelieve, but believe."
> —John 20:27

Yang Yi's family could see the difference Christ was making in his life, and they could not help but be drawn to the light. But one sister of his in particular was not so quickly convinced.

Jing Hua could see the dramatic change in her brother's life, yes. But that change in and of itself hardly seemed enough to push her over the edge into belief.

Jing Hua was a skeptic, after all. She was kind and gentle, but skeptical still the same.

"If God is good," she would ask my wife, "then how can God allow bad things to happen to people all over the world?"

For Jing Hua, this was no scholarly debate in the comforts of an Ivy League college campus. She knew suffering up close and personal. Jing Hua's own family had been dirt-poor. Oftentimes, they would eat one meal a day when she was growing up, and even then, there wasn't always enough rice to go around. Her oldest brother, Yang Yi, would sometimes skip meals just so his younger siblings wouldn't have to miss theirs.

And Jing Hua? She was literally born at home, with no one else around at the time except her mother, as the family was busy working out in the fields that day. Her mom, left with no choice, had to cut her own umbilical cord with a kitchen knife.

Almost two decades later, the kitchen knife, as it were, kept cutting. But now the sharp blade seemed to slash deeper and deeper into Jing Hua's very soul.

Was Jing Hua beyond hope? Were her doubts too strong and too many?

My wife and I kept praying for Jing Hua, even as we continued to meet with her and discuss the Bible.

Finally, after much time and fervent wrestling of spirit, Jing Hua confessed Jesus as Lord. I baptized her in a local river, with my wife Jamey and her brother Yang Yi at my side.

The young Jing Hua, once so full of darkness and doubt, soon began to shine with bright gospel light. Jing Hua's best friend in college, Mei Li, came to faith through her witness. (Mei Li was the first in her family to believe in Jesus.)

In an even more unlikely twist, another of Jing Hua's friends—a guy named Xu—came to faith in Christ through Jing Hua's faithful witness. And Jing Hua eventually married him.

The Lord had truly captured Jing Hua's heart. But there were yet more young hearts to capture.

Chapter 5

Lunch in the Canteen

For God, who said, "Let light shine out of darkness," has shone in our hearts to give the light of the knowledge of the glory of God in the face of Jesus Christ.
—2 Cor. 4:6

Xin Yan was one of the first people my wife and I met when we touched down in China. Xin Yan was an English student at the local university where we came to study Chinese. Her English was really good. In fact, her English was so good, the university's foreign affairs office "assigned" her to be our guide those first few days after we arrived.

Xin Yan was friendly and kind and spent no little time helping us find our way around the city. She took us to the local supermarkets, department stores, and bank, interpreting both the language and the culture at every stop—and laughing with us as we blundered our way through new adventures living in a new place. Xin Yan became the kind of friend we could call anytime with any and all our questions and curiosities.

For our part, we gave Xin Yan an up-close, regular, real-life opportunity to practice her oral English with Americans, not simply the canned, classroom-only, academia sort of study most Chinese are used to. Xin Yan could ask us questions regarding any topic, and we would give her our honest-to-goodness answers—all in English.

Oftentimes, the three of us would eat meals together and chat about life in general. My wife regularly invited Xin Yan and her friends to come over to our tiny campus apartment to bake cookies and other sweet treats. For our first Christmas party, Xin Yan was there. For Easter, the same.

Meanwhile, through all our endeavors and interactions with Xin Yan, we were intentional to talk about our love for Christ. Xin Yan was not so familiar with Christianity at the time. Yet when we chatted about matters of faith, she listened politely and asked good questions.

One spring morning, just before sunrise, as I was praying and reading my Bible, I felt like God wanted me and my wife to go and have dinner with Xin Yan that day. I mentioned this inkling to my wife, and she immediately text messaged Xin Yan to see if she was available that evening. Sure enough, Xin Yan was free for dinner.

So around six o'clock, the three of us met at the campus canteen. The dining hall was packed wall-to-wall with students. Silver-topped rectangle tables lined the cafeteria in perfect rows, with four students seated at each table. The buzz of chatter filled the air, drowning out the sound of young people smacking their rice and vegetables.

With trays in hand while weaving our way through the sea of students and trying not to spill our vast piles of rice, we came upon a recently cleared table. We plopped down our trays, took our seats in the inflexible metal chairs, and began to munch on our meal.

I don't exactly remember how the dinner conversation started. Did we discuss Xin Yan's day, our day, her weekend plans, our weekend plans, or what? I really don't know.

All I know is that my wife very quickly moved the dialogue in a spiritual direction. Jamey began rehearsing for Xin Yan the central claims of the Christian faith—God made man, man sinned against God, Christ died on the cross in our place and rose again, and so on.

This wasn't the first time Jamey and Xin Yan talked through the gospel message in the seven months we knew her. Indeed, they had discussed the Bible on numerous occasions. But it marked the first time that lights began to turn on in Xin Yan's heart and mind. Soon, maybe ten minutes into their back-and-forth exchange, Xin

Yan blurted out, "You mean that Jesus is the bridge between me and God? Is this really true? Because if this is true, this is the best news I've ever heard!"

Beaming with excitement, Xin Yan continued: "It's like I was drowning underwater, but someone pulled me out, and now I can breathe again."

Her water analogy didn't end there. A few weeks later, I baptized Xin Yan, my new sister in Christ, with Jamey at my side, in a nearby river.

Chapter 6

Study Break Tears

> Continue steadfastly in prayer, being
> watchful in it with thanksgiving.
> —Col. 4:2

Jamey and I had just arrived in China. We were acclimating as a couple into our new city. We were language students at the local university. Given that I had spent time in China previously, we were at different language levels. This meant we weren't studying language in the same classroom at the same time with the same teacher. Sometimes our language lessons were in the morning; sometimes our lessons were in the afternoon. Seldom did our schedules match.

On one particular morning, Jamey went to her language class while I stayed back at our apartment and prepared for my afternoon lessons.

That day I was working on my vocabulary flashcards, trying to cram into my head all the new words I was learning. The words weren't exactly sticking to my memory, which meant it was time to press pause on my morning studies and take a breather.

Then suddenly—almost out of nowhere—I felt a strong impression of the Lord that I needed to pray for Jamey. Pray for her; how I didn't know.

Was my wife needing a boost in her studies like I needed in mine? Was there a problem on campus?

Maybe it was nothing. I really had no clue. But I knew I needed to pray.

So I got down on my knees on the cold tile floor of my living room, turning my body and leaning up against the hard wooden couch, hands spread out, and flashcards now set aside. I pleaded with the God of heaven to help my wife and work through her for his own glory.

Moments later, I rose to my feet and glanced at my watch. It was 10:50 a.m.

Reenergized by prayer, I pulled out my flashcards and gave it another go at memorizing. About an hour later, my cell phone rang. It was Jamey.

"You'll never guess what just happened this morning." Her voice bubbled with enthusiasm. "I'm so excited. I met someone today. I'll tell you all about it when I get home."

A short while later, Jamey burst through the front door, still oozing with excitement.

"Honey, you'll never believe this," she said. "During one of my class breaks this morning, I left the classroom and went into the hallway to get a drink of water and go to the bathroom. As I started making my way back to the classroom, a young lady stopped me and introduced herself. Her name is Yi Nuo. She asked me my name and if I was an American."

"And?" I asked, motioning my hands. I assumed there must be more.

"And she asked me if I was a Christian. I said yes. She then told me the story of how she was converted to Christ. Turns out, a few years ago, there was a couple from Europe who had come here to do research at the university. They were Christians, and they shared the gospel with Yi Nuo, and she believed. They helped her study the Bible, but eventually they returned to their homeland."

"Wow! That's awesome!" I said.

"Yeah," Jamey said, "and that's not all. Yi Nuo told me that she's been praying for quite some time that God would bring more Christians from abroad, like this previous couple, who could help her study the Bible and grow as a Christian. I think God answered Yi

Nuo's prayer today. Needless to say, we stood in the hallway, hugging and crying."

At that moment, it occurred to me that perhaps God had answered my prayer, too.

"Dear, what time this morning did you meet Yi Nuo?" I asked.

"Well, let me think," Jamey said. "I met Yi Nuo in the hallway during the study break just before my 11:00 class. So probably sometime between 10:50 and 11:00. Why?"

"Amazing," I replied. "That's the exact same time I stopped and prayed for you. I was memorizing my vocab earlier when, all of a sudden, I felt like I needed to pause and pray for you—I didn't know why, but now I do. That was around 10:50. God really answered right away!"

More right-away answers to prayer were on the way.

Chapter 7

Lord of the Locusts

> Ask, and it will be given to you; seek, and you will find; knock, and it will be opened to you.
> —Matt. 7:7

Jamey and I have always had a special heart for orphans. In God's providence, there was an orphanage in our city. One day, the Lord put it on Jamey's heart to bless the orphanage with some copies of her favorite storybook Bible. But even though we had copies of that particular storybook Bible in Mandarin, we knew that many of the orphans—and even some of the orphanage workers—were illiterate and thus would not be able to read the storybook. So we decided we would make an audio recording in Mandarin, with ding sounds for every turn of the page, so that the children could follow along in the picture book and hear the story in their own language.

Of course, our own Chinese language skills were hardly fluent at this point. We would need someone else's voice for the recording.

Enter again: Yi Nuo.

Yi Nuo, a fairly recent convert to Christianity, was a supersmart young lady. She was working on her graduate degree in linguistics when my wife and I first met her. Yi Nuo could speak multiple languages and had helped edit an ethnic language dictionary.

So when God put it on Jamey's heart to do this project, Yi Nuo was the obvious choice, if she were available.

Jamey shared her idea with Yi Nuo, who quickly agreed to help.

Late one evening, the two of them gathered at Yi Nuo's campus apartment. They used a digital recorder and began recording Yi Nut's voice as she read the Bible stories from the book, one page after another. But soon Jamey and Yi Nuo encountered a problem.

It was the season for locusts. And the noise of the locusts was loud. Really loud. So loud was their hum, blaring through the windows of the apartment, that it drowned out the sound of Yi Nuo's voice on the recorder.

"The locusts are so loud!" Yi Nuo exclaimed. "What shall we do?"

The two ladies paused and looked at each other, wondering if they could outlast the insects' untimely interruption.

"They don't seem to be slowing down," Jamey replied.

"No," Yi Nuo said. "But when else are we going to record the stories?"

Yi Nuo could scarcely hide her look of concern. It was hard enough getting this meeting arranged in the first place. With all of Yi Nuo's classes and various academic commitments, it was highly unlikely that Jamey and Yi Nuo would be able to reschedule another meeting anytime soon.

"Hey, let's not lose heart," Jamey said. "God is bigger than locusts. He is powerful and can cause them to quiet down."

"You really think so?" Yi Nuo asked.

"Of course!" Jamey said emphatically, though it quickly dawned on her that she had never prayed for the silencing of locusts before.

O Lord, please help us! Jamey's quick prayer before the prayer certainly felt desperate. *What will Yi Nuo think if you don't answer?*

The two of them closed their eyes, lowered their heads, and each prayed.

Moments later, after they finished praying, they lifted their heads and opened their eyes.

"Listen!" Yi Nuo squealed. "The locusts—they are silent! God answered our prayers!"

Yi Nuo resumed her reading of the Bible stories, and the pair was able to complete the recording project that evening while the locusts kept quiet.

"God is truly great," Yi Nuo would later say. "I feel so encouraged that he granted our request."

And God did more than grant their request. Shortly thereafter, Jamey and Yi Nuo were able to present multiple copies of the storybook and an audio recording CD to the orphanage.

Chapter 8

The Problem Solver's Wide Web

> And also for me, that words may be given to me in opening my mouth boldly to proclaim the mystery of the gospel.
>
> —Eph. 6:19

Professor Fen is not likely to grace the cover of *People* magazine. Nor is she likely to be named *Time* magazine's Person of the Year. Yet her personal influence and life's legacy are certainly known to the Lord and to those who know her well.

Born in a humble small town, Professor Fen worked hard in school, earned her college degree, and later landed a teaching position at the local university. But before she began her tenure at an institution for higher learning, she owned and operated a small bookshop near the university campus. One day a mysterious visitor brought her a bag of books, free of charge, and simply said, "These books will sell well." The man delivering the books offered no further explanation and promptly disappeared.

Professor Fen opened the cloth sack and discovered a bundle of Bibles. She was not familiar with the Bible—she'd never even seen one before. But lo and behold, she marked them for sale, and the Bibles sold like hotcakes. Curious at these fast-moving sales items, she read the Bible for herself and shortly thereafter became a Christian.

By the time I met Professor Fen, she had long since sold her bookshop and joined the faculty at the local university—and was a strong, committed Christian. Every chance she had, Professor Fen seized the opportunity to share the good news with her students. Moreover, she was a fantastic networker. My wife and I called her our "problem solver." If we ever ran into a snag of any kind, all we had to do was call her, and she would immediately direct us to someone in her vast web of contacts who could crack the code. But in all her networking, Professor Fen always acted very deliberately in order to connect believers with unbelievers.

Her own family was a prime example of this. When my wife and I first met Professor Fen, her husband and son were not yet believers. So she quickly introduced us to them—in hopes that we would influence them for Christ. Eventually, both her husband and her son came to faith in Jesus. Also, Professor Fen was friends with a very prominent painter in China—again, he was not a believer at first—and introduced us to him. Eventually, the famous artist also professed faith in the Lord Jesus. This sort of connection and Christ-impacting consequence happened again and again.

It was through Professor Fen that I actually had the opportunity to guest-speak at a provincial high school for internet addicts. The school, several hours away by car from my city of residence, was comprised exclusively of students whose parents had enrolled them there due to their excessive internet gaming habits. The principal of the school, not himself a believer, was willing to let me, a believer, interact with his students in the hopes that something—*anything*—would change their outlook on life. This afforded me an amazing opportunity to openly share my Christian faith with the students.

Yet as amazed as I was by that opportunity, nothing could prepare me for my next surprise.

Chapter 9

The Lecture Hall

As indeed in the whole world it is bearing fruit and increasing.
—Col. 1:6

One day while walking and talking on the university campus with one of my Chinese friends, Bo, an English student, I made the offhanded comment that someday, if ever given the opportunity, I would love to give a onetime lecture presentation on the Bible's influence on the West.

"After all," I said, "the Bible has made a profound impact on Western culture—you know, on literature, music, the sciences, and much more. I think that would be very interesting, don't you think?"

"Sure," Bo said, nodding obligingly. And we moved on to the next subject, neither of us really giving it a second notice. Or so I thought.

A few weeks later, my cell phone rang. It was my friend, Bo.

"Do you remember when you mentioned giving a lecture on the Bible's influence on the West? Were you serious about that?"

"Um. Well, yeah, I think so," I said. "What's up?"

"I just chatted with one of our university administrators," Bo said. "I told him your idea. He really liked it. He wants you to give your lecture presentation in two weeks. Do it all in English in the big lecture hall. You get ninety minutes, not one minute under or over."

"Wait, what? Are you serious?" I was totally taken aback. "I mean, this is great and all. But is this a joke?"

"I'm serious," he said. "You'll need a PPT. Plan to wear a suit. Oh, and one last thing. Our leader says—no talking like a priest. Got it?"

Not talking like a priest? Shoot, I'm not Catholic, I thought to myself. *What a deal!*

"Got it," I said.

For the next two weeks, I prayed, prepped, and prayed some more. I fine-tuned and timed my presentation and checked and rechecked my PPT. And since I didn't own a suit in China, I went and had one tailor-made.

As for the no-priest-talk clause in my verbal agreement, I figured I could still include a carefully crafted gospel message right at the outset of my presentation. I would simply explain, in my introduction, why the subject matter mattered to me. I would plan to openly acknowledge my Christian faith and share something of my own conversion experience—and later connect its meaning to the famous hymn "Amazing Grace" when I got to the part in the presentation about the Bible's influence on Western music.

Yep, I was all ready to go. Except for one minor snag.

Just days before I was scheduled to give my presentation, I received word via my on-campus friends that members of the National Security Bureau (think Chinese FBI) had gotten wind of this activity and were planning to put a stop to it.

So I simply prayed some more. *Lord, if you want this lecture presentation to go forward, put a stop to those who want to stop it.*

Then came the day of the presentation. I wasn't sure if it was still a go or not. I decided I would just show up at the right place and time, all dressed in my suit and tie, with the PPT on my flash disk, and roll with it. I knew it was all in the Lord's hands, even if the feds made a guest appearance and shut it all down.

When I arrived at the lecture hall that evening, the room was bustling with activity. Members of the National Security Bureau were not present. However, most of the Chinese upper-class English majors were. There were one hundred twenty seats in the auditorium.

All were filled. There were no empty seats. An additional thirty or more students stood without chairs, flanking the side aisles.

My presentation promptly began at seven o'clock and ended exactly at eight thirty, with not a single interruption. I was able to clearly articulate the Bible's influence on Western culture and, as planned, weave in the gospel message without sounding like a priest. The school leaders seemed quite pleased and even allowed for a brief Q&A.

After it was all over, the only other foreigner (besides my wife) who attended the lecture came up and spoke with me. Bill, an American English professor and avowed atheist, complimented my presentation and told me that he had encouraged all his students to attend this "good learning opportunity," which they did.

Once again, the Lord found ways to work through unlikely people and circumstances. And he wasn't finished yet.

Chapter 10

A Widow's Awful Food and Awesome Prayers

> Pray without ceasing.
> —1 Thess. 5:17

Sister Ai had earned quite a reputation for her cooking. Without a doubt, of all the widows at the local church, Sister Ai's cooking skills were viewed, hands down, as the worst.

So when the foreign couple (namely, my wife and I) asked leaders of the local church if they would recommend any of their widows to become our house helper to cook and clean as a way to earn a little extra income while giving our young family much-needed relief around the house, everyone was shocked—including the final nominee herself—when Sister Ai got the nod.

"Please pray for me," Sister Ai told her fellow widow friends. "I need God to turn my poor cooking into something delicious."

God must have listened to her prayers.

Jamey and I didn't know about Sister Ai's one-star kitchen rating when we first hired her to come and prepare our lunchtime meals. On the contrary, we thought Sister Ai's cooking tasted fabulous, especially her fried dumplings.

But even still, what impressed us most about Sister Ai was her ever-joyful spirit. No matter what we asked her to do—regardless of how mundane or messy the task—Sister Ai did all things with a thankful attitude, always praising the Lord and praying as she worked.

One day, as our two boys were playing in the living room, our son Ethan, who was one at the time and barely walking, tripped and fell. His forehead smashed against the edge of a hard plastic cup on the floor and split the skin wide open right between his eyes.

I was not at home at the time, as I was away in a village somewhere, doing the work of an evangelist. So Jamey, as soon as she heard Ethan's loud scream, came rushing into the room, as did Sister Ai. Jamey immediately snatched up Ethan from the floor, examined his bleeding forehead, and began to apply pressure with a towel.

In the midst of caring for Ethan, Jamey heard a low voice in the background but paid no attention to it. However, after ensuring that Ethan's bleeding had slowed down, Jamey turned around, still holding him in her arms, and noticed, to her amazement, Sister Ai on the floor, face down on her knees and praying, asking the Lord for help to stop the flow of blood. Next to Sister Ai lay our other son. Elijah, whom we had named after the Old Testament prophet, was also kneeling face down on the floor in a praying position, mimicking Sister Ai.

Eventually, Jamey and Sister Ai took Ethan to the local ER, where he received several stitches for his head wound. Everything turned out okay. The injury to Ethan's head only left a minimal physical scar. And yet that incident—which involved an unlikely widow and her bright example of prayer—left an indelible impression on my wife for years to come.

Chapter 11

Life-Changing Pepsi

The heart of man plans his way, but the Lord establishes his steps.
—Prov. 16:9

The summer heat magnified the weariness we felt in our languishing bodies as my missionary colleague and I walked down endless dusty roads in and out of far-flung villages.

Our worn-out feet and sun-scorched faces begged for rest, yet our hearts believed God was far from finished for the day.

Still, we needed something to whet our tongues if we were to keep pressing forward on the arduous journey. As we neared the next village, my friend Robert and I spotted a small shop, barely removed from the beaten path.

"Surely they'll have something to drink," I said, squinting in the sun as I spoke.

"Yep, they usually do," Robert replied.

We entered the humble shop, with its few rows of mostly stocked shelves staring at us and the shopkeeper walking toward us.

"Ni yao mai shenme?" the short middle-aged man asked in his thick but still understandable countryside accent.

"What do you want to buy?"

I immediately responded. *"Women yao mai he de dongxi."*

"We want to buy something to drink."

If our ability as foreigners to communicate so easily with the shopkeeper surprised him, he didn't let his surprise distract from the sale. He quickly pointed to a small freezer case to his right.

"*Zai nali,*" he said, motioning his hand.

"Over there."

We walked over to the small freezer case, gently opened the lid, and immediately felt refreshed as we gazed at its cold contents. There lay before us several semi-chilly, twenty-ounce bottles of Pepsi.

Glorious day, I thought to myself. *And I don't even like Pepsi. But I'll gladly drink Pepsi today. Thank you, Lord!*

We paid for our Pepsis and stood there at the entrance of the small shop, with cold drinks in hand, enjoying a brief reprieve from the sweaty midafternoon heat.

Suddenly, we heard a female voice holler in our direction.

"*Hallow!*"

Passing us on the street—and pausing for our response—was a teenage girl.

"*Hallow!*" The young lady repeated her happy, albeit distorted "hello" a second time.

"Hello!" I chanted back, waving my free hand.

"Where are you from?" the girl asked.

Careful to annunciate my every word, I replied, "We are from America."

"Oh," she said. "Nice to meet you."

"Nice to meet you too," I said, supposing that short greeting would be the full extent of our cross-cultural exchange. These brief courtesy hellos happened to me all the time in China—certainly nothing to write home about. Except that this particular hello didn't end at hello, which is why her next question surprised me.

"Do you want to visit my home?" Her invitation intrigued me.

"Your home?" I asked, a bit sheepishly. "Where is your home?" I wasn't sure if it mattered. Would my missionary colleague and I—two young men—follow a teenage girl to her house? That sure didn't seem to me like wise missionary methodology. However, my mulling over the subject was quickly interrupted.

"Over there." The girl pointed to a tiny house around the corner from the shop where we stood. "Come on," she said. "I'll show you."

Robert and I looked at each other and shrugged with resignation.

"Alrighty then," I said. "Let's go."

We followed her to a small house catercorner to the shop. The dwelling was simple but clean. We sat down on miniature wooden stools at the inside entrance of her home. We really weren't sure who all lived there—it was quiet when we arrived—but I knew we wouldn't stay long.

So I cut to the chase and switched from English to Chinese. "I want to tell you some stories from my favorite book," I said.

Her eyes lit up as she heard me speak in her native tongue. I began with creation in Genesis and then shared some of Jesus' miracles.

A few minutes into my monologue, I stopped. "Have you ever heard these stories before?" I asked, expecting her to say no. After all, we were deep in the boonies. Pepsi made it out here, sure. But the gospel—not so much.

"Yes," she said. "I've heard some of these stories before. My teacher told them to me."

"*Zhen de ma?*" I exclaimed. *Are you serious?*

"Yes," she said, surprised by my surprise. "Would you like to meet my teacher?"

"Yes, I would," I said, unable to hold back my enthusiasm.

"Okay," she replied. "I will introduce you to him."

My introduction to her teacher didn't happen on the same day. But the introduction would come soon enough, and it would be well worth the wait.

Chapter 12

The Gospel in Leviticus

And beginning with Moses and all the Prophets, he interpreted to them in all the Scriptures the things concerning himself.
—Luke 24:27

A couple weeks after my providential Pepsi encounter, I received a text message from the young gal's teacher, Mr. Ma, asking if I had time to meet with him.

"Of course," I replied.

I arranged to meet Mr. Ma for dinner at a restaurant in a county town not far from the village middle school where he taught.

When my missionary colleague and I arrived at the restaurant, a slender, thirtysomething young man wearing a red basketball jersey t-shirt and athletic shorts immediately approached us.

"You must be Matt and Robert. Nice to meet you. My name is Ma Yize. Please come with me."

We shook hands and then followed Mr. Ma to a private room at the back of the restaurant.

"Do you like spicy food?" he asked, directing us with his outstretched hands to have a seat at the large lazy Susan–topped table before us.

"Sure," we replied.

Without delay, a waitress brought out soup-sized bowls, packed them tightly with white rice, and filled our cups with tea. Moments later, the same petite food server blanketed the round table with various meat and vegetable dishes, each cuisine slightly tented with its own red pepper glow.

We picked up our chopsticks and began to eat. It was a fine meal indeed. Yet the savory flavors could not distract us from our main purpose in gathering.

So, laying my chopsticks across my bowl and folding my hands, my chin resting on my knuckles, I stared directly at Mr. Ma and got to the point.

"My friend here and I are both Christians," I said. "We follow Jesus. Our favorite book is the Bible. It seems you are familiar with this important book. Please tell me—how do you know stories from the Bible?"

Mr. Ma leaned into the table, paused for a brief second as if to weigh his words, then leaned back in his chair.

"A few years ago," he said, "I was teaching geography to my middle school students, and we were studying different countries and cultures. One day, while searching on the internet, I found an article about Christianity. I read the article and became very curious."

"Curious?" I asked.

"Curious about Christianity and the Bible. So I found a Bible online and began to read it," he said.

"What did you read in the Bible?"

Mr. Ma didn't seem bothered by my barrage of questions.

"I started at the beginning," he said, "and I just kept reading." Mr. Ma rehearsed for us something of Genesis and the creation account, Leviticus and the sacrificial system, as well as Isaiah and the suffering servant, all in clear but less precise terms.

"You mean to tell us you read the entire Old Testament?" I asked. "Did you understand it?"

"Not exactly." Mr. Ma let out a light laugh. "But as I told you, I kept reading. And when I began to read the New Testament, I discovered that Jesus was the fulfillment of everything I had been reading about in the Old Testament. I realized Jesus was the Lamb of God who took our sin upon himself. So I believed in Jesus."

"Wait—what?" I interjected. "Are you telling us that you're a Christian?"

Mr. Ma smiled. "Yes, but I've never known another Christian before. You're the first Christians I've ever met."

I all but leaped across the table to hug my new brother in Christ.

"What about your students?" I asked. "I guess you've been telling Bible stories to your students?"

"Yes," he said. "I've also been telling my coworkers."

I nearly gasped. "You've been telling a lot of people, then?"

"Yes," he said, "but I feel a little bad." Mr. Ma's eyes flashed to the floor.

"You feel a little bad—why? I don't understand."

Mr. Ma explained, "Well, recently I bought ten copies of the Bible on the internet to give away to my coworkers, and I've only given away five so far."

"Brother Ma," I said, my eyes filling with tears, "I don't think you need to feel bad about only giving away five Bibles. God is going to use you to enlarge his kingdom, one planted seed at a time."

Little did I know that one of those seeds was soon set to sprout.

Chapter 13

A Taoist Finds Truth

> All the ends of the earth shall remember
> and turn to the Lord,
> and all the families of the nations
> shall worship before you.
> —Psalm 22:27

Brother Ma had a zeal for sharing the Word with others. But first and foremost, he had a zeal for obeying the Word himself. Not long after I initially met Brother Ma, he made a keen observation based on his reading of the Book of Acts.

"I noticed the early Christians were baptized as soon as they believed in Jesus," he said. "So when can I be baptized?"

"Well, that's a good question," I retorted, half-embarrassed that Brother Ma had brought up the subject of baptism before I could. "If you believe that Jesus is the Son of God who died on the cross for your sins and rose again on the third day, then I don't see any reason why you can't be baptized."

"I believe," he said. At this point, I didn't need to hear those magical words to feel assured that Brother Ma was a genuine follower of Jesus—I already knew.

A week or so later, when we met at a local river to baptize Brother Ma, he was accompanied by his friend and coworker, Mr. Ng. Mr. Ng, a middle school science teacher, was, by his own declaration, a practicing Taoist. (Taoism is an ancient Chinese religion whose adherents seek to exist in harmony with the universe.)

Mr. Ng said very little, his round face largely expressionless, as he watched his friend go under the water and back up again. As I baptized Brother Ma, I silently asked the Lord to capture Mr. Ng's heart.

A few weeks after the baptism, I received a phone call from Brother Ma.

His voice, always so full of energy, seemed particularly happy that day.

"Mr. Ng and I are in town today," he said, "and Mr. Ng would like to chat with you. Are you at home now?"

"Yes, I am at home," I said. "Come on over."

When the two men arrived, I invited them to have a seat in my living room.

Not one to dance around the point, I jumped right in. "What can I do for you guys?" I asked.

Brother Ma immediately spoke up. "As you know, I've been telling Mr. Ng all about Jesus. I recently gave him a Bible, and he's been reading it."

Mr. Ng nodded in affirmation as Brother Ma continued, "And now he wants to believe and be baptized."

Brother Ma paused, as if waiting for my response.

"Wow!" I said, stumbling for words. "That's really great, Mr. Ng."

No doubt, I was thrilled, but I wasn't quite sure what to say. So I figured I'd let Mr. Ng speak for himself.

"Why do you want to become a Christian?" I asked him.

Mr. Ng, now ready to open his mouth, sat up straight in his chair, his round face lighting up as he spoke.

"As I've been reading the Bible, I've discovered that there is one Creator, God, who made everything. He made mankind, starting with one man and one woman. He put them in the garden and gave them a command. But the man and woman disobeyed. They sinned against God by breaking his command. By disobeying God's command, sin entered the world. This meant ruin and misery for the world. All have sinned against God, and all are separated from God."

I could hardly believe what I was hearing—such depth of understanding. It felt like Mr. Ng was walking with me down the Romans Road—and *he* was the tour guide. Mr. Ng went on.

"But God had a plan all along. Two thousand years ago, God sent his Son, Jesus, to come to earth. Jesus was perfect. He never sinned. Jesus willingly sacrificed his life on the cross to pay the penalty for our sins—for my sins."

Mr. Ng paused. "I have believed in Jesus for the forgiveness of my sins. I want to follow Jesus as Lord. And for my first step of following him, I want to be baptized."

Again, I was floored by his grasp of the gospel.

So off to the local river we went once again. This time it was Brother Ma doing the baptizing—with me merely assisting—as his friend and coworker Brother Ng went under the water and back up again.

I started meeting regularly with these two brothers for Bible study, prayer, and worship. Mr. Ng's wife frequently sat in and observed our weekly gatherings, mostly without a word. But eventually she too confessed Jesus Christ as Lord, and it was her husband who baptized her.

The Lord was capturing the hearts of China's next generation, one Mr. Ma and one Mr. Ng at a time. But God still had a heart for China's older generation, also. And he would get the gospel to them as well, even those living in the most remote and out-of-the-way places.

Chapter 14

Uncle W and the Dogs

And your ears shall hear a word behind you, saying,
"This is the way, walk in it," when you turn to
the right or when you turn to the left.
—Isa. 30:21

I was never one to be a big fan of hiking. Fair-skinned and ready to sunburn at the drop of a hat—literally—I did not much care for long mountain treks. Yet it was my firm conviction in my decade overseas that I would do whatever it took to get the gospel to faraway places for people who needed to hear it.

If that meant hiking to remote villages, then so be it.

One day, my wife and I set out to go to one such remote place. We had never been to that particular place before. I simply saw it on the map and felt led by the Lord to travel there, praying that God would open doors for the Word to go forth.

So we hopped on a bus and made our way in that direction. However, at some point along the path, the bus unexpectedly stopped—this was the end of the road for buses. Any forward progress would have to come on foot.

Jamey and I looked at each other and shrugged as we exited the vehicle.

"Let's get ready to walk," I said cautiously, not sure if my wife would share in my newfound enthusiasm.

The two of us walked on a winding, uphill dirt road for a solid hour or more. We kept thinking that at any moment, a village would suddenly pop up in front of us. But no such village popped up. Now, normally, an hour of walking wasn't really all that long—my wife and I had done longer hikes before. But for some reason, the ambiguity of our current location and its exact distance to our final destination made us less patient—less patient with each other and less patient with the Lord.

As we neared the next small bridge—*surely a bridge indicates proximity to people, right?*—we stopped for a breather.

"We need to pray," declared my wife, "and ask the Lord to give us wisdom whether to keep pushing ahead or turn back."

Taking my seat on a ledge next to the bridge and Jamey taking her seat next to me, I cupped my left hand on top of her right hand and began to pray.

"Lord, we need your help." My petition wasn't particularly memorable. I actually don't recall what I said in my prayer. I just remember that as I prayed, I felt a strong sense in my soul that we needed to push ahead and not turn back.

"Honey," I said, after saying amen, "I really think we're supposed to keep pressing ahead."

Jamey's eyes screamed skepticism, even though her lips said nothing. As we plowed forward, our dusty path climbed higher and higher into the lonely mountains. One bend of the road doubled up after another, with brush on every side waving as we wormed our way up the trail. Finally, we came upon a tiny clearing beyond the woods. A single house, with stone steps leading up to it, stood at a distance.

Suddenly a pack of three mangy, tan-colored dogs burst out into the open, as though released from a cage, and headed straight toward us, barking at full volume. Then, just as quickly as the dogs appeared, an older man, short but sturdy in stature, also appeared, calling the mad guardians back to their stations. The fierce animals complied, even if reluctantly.

Taken aback but equally thankful, I hollered out to the man in his own language, offering a friendly greeting. Delighted that his new visitor could speak his own tribal tongue—a native tongue quite different from Mandarin, mind you—the man of the house gladly welcomed the two of us into his humble abode.

The man—Uncle W, as we later came to call him—asked us about our nationality and family origins, and we shared basic introductions for just a bit. But the polite pleasantries didn't last long, as I soon cut to the chase.

"The Most High God has sent me to you," I said. "I bring you a message of good news." Uncle W didn't take his eyes off me as I worked my way through the grand narrative of Scripture—in his tribal tongue—and explained to him the story of redemption. As I zoomed in on Christ and the cross, I exhorted Uncle W to repent of his sins and believe in Jesus.

"Do you believe?" I asked him.

"Yes." Uncle W's straightforward answer shocked me. In fact, I was so surprised by his childlike response that I turned to my wife, who was sitting next to me, and asked her to share the gospel with him in Mandarin, thinking perhaps Uncle W could not actually understand my tribal tongue and was simply nodding in confusion rather than in genuine affirmation.

So Jamey shared the gospel with Uncle W, this time in her and his second language, Mandarin. When, in her proclamation, my wife got to the cross and the resurrection, she likewise called Uncle W to repent and believe in Jesus.

"Do you believe?" Jamey asked him.

"Yes! Yes, I do!" Uncle W seemed almost annoyed that she even had to ask. "I understood it the first time when your husband told me," he said. "I believe."

After a few follow-up visits with Uncle W, who was age sixty-seven at the time, I accompanied him down a mountain slope on a cool but sunny Saturday, found a river, and baptized my new brother in Christ the day before Easter.

Chapter 15

The Summit

Go therefore and make disciples of all nations, baptizing them in the name of the Father and of the Son and of the Holy Spirit.
—Matt. 28:19

The room in the high-rise building overlooking one of China's oldest cities contained almost no empty chairs. Three or four dozen Chinese Christians sat in their seats with razor-sharp focus as they listened to more than a few testimonies of God's mercy poured out on their homeland.

Key leaders from the region's underground church network had gathered to pray and strategize concerning the next steps in their desire to better reach the lost in their prefecture and province for Christ.

I was specially invited to this meeting, perhaps in part because it was known in some circles that I was actively ministering among an unreached people group in a different part of China, and they thought it would be profitable for me to share certain aspects of my experience.

As I prepared to take my stand at the small podium, I couldn't help but soak in the scene. A generation or two previously, this gathering would have been thought unimaginable. And yet here we were, one small thread in a much larger tapestry, a group of spiritually mature brothers and sisters with one heart and mind, dedicated to the advance of the gospel.

"You know the Great Commission," I said, my voice somber yet confident. "Christ has called us to make disciples of all nations. He has called you—all of you—to this great task. God will help you. He will be your strength."

Indeed, from coast to coast in China, from province to province, north, east, south, and west, God is raising a multitude of Christians, hungry and thirsty for His Word, committed to the Great Commission, and eager to see Christ's kingdom extend to the utter parts of the globe. Without a doubt, God is helping his people. He is giving them strength.

Chapter 16

Flashback: Blindsided by God's Grace

> But I do not account my life of any value nor as precious to myself, if only I may finish my course and the ministry that I received from the Lord Jesus, to testify to the gospel of the grace of God.
> —Acts 20:24

When God first put China on my heart many years ago, I felt it was my destiny to go to China as a missionary. But going from heart to destiny is not always a straight line.

With one year left in college, I was determined to get to China as soon as I walked across the stage with my undergraduate diploma. But in the meantime, I would need to find a mission-sending agency. So I did. In the fall of my senior year, I went online, did my research, and submitted my application to a reputable and well-known agency. In fairly short order, the agency mailed me an invitation letter, asking me to come for an interview right after the New Year. That January, I flew out to their agency headquarters, discussed potential job assignments, and was interviewed by several members of their staff.

All was going well, it seemed—until it wasn't.

On the last full day of interviews, in my final one-on-one interview, a tall brown-haired somewhat serious-looking man sat across from me with a clipboard in his left hand.

The questions were many, but none seemed difficult. I felt my answers were solid. I thought we were done, and all was well.

But then the man cleared his throat.

"I'm going to be really honest with you," he said, partially resting the clipboard on his knee. "I really like you. You're a nice guy."

He went on. "But your eyes are going to be an issue overseas."

Instantly, I knew what he meant. In fact, I dreaded that someone somewhere might say that. And here it was.

You see, I've been legally blind for most of my life. I was diagnosed with glaucoma at age eight. The eye disease, which likely went undetected for some time, severely damaged my optic nerve, which consequently diminished my eyesight. As such, my peripheral vision, even in my better eye, cannot be corrected with glasses. The glasses I do wear only help for reading up close. I cannot drive a car. Indeed, there are a lot of things I cannot do because of my "eye issues."

So I could hardly blame this guy for thinking I would not be able to last—much less thrive—overseas. I mean, there's no getting around my disability. I can't deny that the obstacles are real.

"Listen," he said. "I'm not saying you absolutely won't be accepted into our program. I'm just saying, don't be surprised if you get a rejection letter."

Needless to say, I left the interview not a little dejected.

As I flew back to Oklahoma and began my final spring semester of college, I wondered if maybe I had made a mistake with the whole overseas mission thing. Over the next week or two, I mulled over other postgraduation options—all stateside.

Maybe the Lord will just have me stay here in America, I thought.

But the Lord had other thoughts.

One evening, when I went to the university mailroom to retrieve my mail, I found a manila envelope from the missions sending agency with whom I had just recently interviewed.

The envelope sure is thick to be a rejection letter, I reasoned. I rushed to my dorm room and tore open the contents.

I had been accepted! Against all human odds, I was on my way to China.

And sure enough, by God's amazing grace, I not only lasted in China—despite my real physical handicap—but I also thrived. Young men, old men, college students, postgraduate students, village teachers, famous artists, and many more heard and believed the gospel. Entire families—some the first in their villages to embrace Christ—were transformed by the message of hope and redemption. Lives were impacted. The Lord Jesus was honored. And as for me, I got to see with my own imperfect eyes Christ's triumph in China as many spiritual eyes were opened to behold his glorious grace.

About the Author

Matt Click spent ten years in China. He lived in multiple provinces, studied Mandarin, and traveled in and out of countless cities and villages, sharing the gospel everywhere he went. Since returning to the USA, he has pastored churches in Oklahoma and Kansas. He currently serves as an elder at Vine Community Church in El Dorado, a small town northeast of Wichita. More of his writings, as well as his contact information, can be found at VictoryNotDefeat.com.